FIRST PRESBYT

D0098144

A Homemaker Talks with God

TOO BUSY
> not
TO PRAY

Jo Carr & Imogene Sorley

Abingdon   •   Nashville

TOO BUSY NOT TO PRAY

Copyright © 1966 by Abingdon Press

All rights in this book are reserved.
No part of the book may be reproduced in any
manner whatsoever without written permission of
the publisher except brief quotations embodied in
critical articles or reviews. For information address
Abingdon, Nashville, Tennessee.

ISBN 0-687-42379-1
Library of Congress Catalog Card Number: 66-10853

"First Thanksgiving Prayer," p. 63, by Jo Carr, reprinted from *Primary Teaching Pictures*, © 1962
by The Methodist Publishing House. "Prayer
For A Child," p. 64, by Jane Merchant, reprinted
from *Together* Magazine, © 1956 by Lovick Pierce.
Poetry on p. 84 is from "To A Waterfowl," by Wil-
liam Cullen Bryant. "Spirit of the Living God,"
p. 80, used by permission of Daniel Iverson. Poetry
on p. 51 is by St. Patrick.

MANUFACTURED BY THE PARTHENON PRESS AT
NASHVILLE, TENNESSEE, UNITED STATES OF AMERICA

To Galen and Gene

FOREWORD

The pages have been written to help meet the devotional needs of young homemakers. Instead of a collection of thoughtful meditations, this is a book of prayer, and of prayers. They are not the traditional prayers of the church, for the most part, but the crying out of us "part-time" Christians who seek something more real.

The unconventional approach is not just for the sake of being unconventional. Sometimes saying something in a new and startling way is the simplest shortcut to the mind of the reader. It makes her *notice* what was said.

The book is written to help us modern women, most of whom have not been trained in spiritual matters, to sort out our cluttered thinking and enter into a valid and vital relationship with God.

CONTENTS

A Month of Days 11

My Special Days and Seasons 45
    January 47
    February 48
    February 14 49
    March 50
    March 17 51
    April 52
    April 15 53
    May 54
    Mother's Day 55
    June 56
    July 57
    July 4 58
    August 59
    September 60
    October 61
    November 62
    Thanksgiving 63
    December 64
    Christmas Day 65
    December 26 66
    December 27 67
    Communion Sunday 68
    Birthday 69

Moving Day 70
A Day of Birth 71
A Day of Death 72
Reflection 73
Sunday Morning 74
A Holy Weekday 75
Palm Sunday 76
Maundy Thursday 77
Good Friday 78
Easter Sunday 79
Pentecost 80

My Ordinary Days 81

A MONTH OF DAYS

1st Day

"Just listen—
   God will speak," she said.
   I couldn't see it—shook my head,
   And muttered some amenity.
   God speaks, I know, but not to me.
   He speaks to mystics, saints and seers,
   Just as He has down through the years;
   While I am common clay; and yet,
   Her words I couldn't quite forget.

"Just listen—
   God will speak," she said.
   And I believed, and bowed my head. . . .
   My yearning heart was strangely stirred,
   And in the silent dawn, I heard
   God speak to me.

I heard, Lord. Not with my ears, but with my heart.
In this moment of quiet, I know that thou art with
   me.

Amen.

2nd Day

Lord of all creation,
and Lord of me, too,

sometimes I come to this place of quiet, and try as best
I can to shut out the distractions. I sit here for a
while, and think good thoughts. Then, having done
that, I say "Amen"—and go back to the dailiness of
living without ever having reached thee. I feel no
stronger, no better, no closer to thee than before I
came.

But I am, Lord. I am stronger for having stuck to the
discipline of a time for prayer. I am better for having
quieted my distracted mind for a moment. I am closer
to thee for having reached upward.

Times of prayer are not always the same, and it is not
reasonable for me to expect them to be. Some days I
am more in tune with thee. Those days are blessed
with a heart-stirring assurance that we have been in
conversation together, thee and me. Other days are
duller ones. I come, and I pray, and I know in my
mind that you are near. But I cannot feel your
presence.

Still, I know. I know. For this, too, I give thanks.

Amen.

3rd Day

Listen, Lord! Thy servant speaketh.

I don't have but a minute, so I will have to pray fast. I have a meeting at 10:00, and I promised the kids we could go to the library today. I have to put a roast on for supper, and fix something for dessert. The living room looks like a whirlwind got loose in it—and my ironing basket runneth over. I will have to pray fast, so I can get on with things. So listen, Lord. . . .

All without stopping for breath! Some prayer! I get carried away, Lord. I would like to be a good wife and mother, and I forget that there is more to it than just checking off a list of things to be done. If I mullygrub at the kids all the way to the library, it would be better not to go. Roast served with cold shoulder, or hot tongue, is poor nourishment indeed. And it just might be that my moment with thee is more important than the ironing pile.

Forgive my dither, Lord. In quietness and confidence shall be my strength.

> In quietness.
> A moment with thee.
> Our Father, who is in heaven,
>   holy is thy name.

Speak, Lord, for thy servant heareth.

                    Amen.

4th Day

I just did not understand, Lord. I thought *the presence of God* had to be a blinding vision, and a voice. Like on the Damascus Road.

I could not see any vision, or hear any voice. So I figured we just could not communicate, you and I.

Now, Lord, I began to see a little clearer. Better than visions and voices is this inner warmth that makes me know I am not alone—that makes me aware of being in the presence of God.

I feel it here, but when I turn my back on this quiet place, I *leave* it here! If I could just keep this awareness as I go back to the world of clocks and watches and jobs to be done.

Brother Lawrence could do it—saint that he was! He could scour pots and scrub floors and get the monastery meals on time, and walk with thee—all at once.

Can I? Today? If not all day, can I for a little while? While I wash the breakfast dishes, can I sing thy praise, and sing it from the heart? While I sweep the floor, can I rid my mind of useless clutter? When I sew on buttons, and dust the windowsills, and answer a headful of childish "whys," can I at the same time walk with thee? For thou art with me.

Amen.

5th Day

My least one paused, with conscious grace,
And cleared her throat, and "said" for me
the verse that she had learned today.
I learned it, too, when I was three.
    That God is love.
I never really gave it thought
Until just now—but God above
Who dwells in each of us, is *love*.

O my Father, the reason I get so frustrated is because
I try to harbor feelings and attitudes and reactions
that are incompatible with the divine love within me.
I cannot at the same time resent and relax. I cannot
begrudge and be blessed. Wholeness comes with
rooting out the incompatibles.

If I could be caught up wholly with your love—well,
then there might be things you could *do*, here in my
Jerusalem, using me.

Amen.

6th Day

Lord, we sang it in church, Sunday—
and I had never really seen the words to that second
verse before:

> "I ask no dream, no prophet ecstasies,
>   No sudden rending of the veil of clay,
>   No angel visitant, no opening skies;
>   But take the dimness of my soul away."

That is my prayer. Take the dimness of my soul away.
When it comes to things of the spirit, I see through
a glass, darkly. Dimly. Vaguely.

I look for thee, and my soul's dimness cannot per-
ceive.

I look for light on my own path, that I may know
more surely the way to go. The light is there, but my
soul some days is blind.

Dull and blind. Groping along in a fog, knowing that
the light is there, but too wrapped up in itself to see.

Lord, take the dimness of my soul away.

Amen.

7th Day
A Meditation on the Creed

I believe in God,
    my Father, almighty,
who in his wisdom lets me create my own heaven, or
    less, on earth;
and in Jesus Christ, his Son, whom he sent to show us
    the way;
    who lived as a man among us,
    and lives now as God within us.
I believe this is his Holy Spirit, this God-within,
whereby even I become a partaker of the divine
    nature,
wherein I find strength and help in my own times
    of need.
I believe in the fellowship of believers here,
and I am aware of the fellowship of saints hereafter.
I believe in the continuation of my life beyond this
    small span of years,
and in the fulfillment of my search, begun here, for
    fellowship with the Father.

Amen, amen.

8th Day

Lord, she sort of shook me up last night when she said her prayers. She knelt there by the bed, squirming a little to get all settled. Then . . . "Thank you for my mother. She 'bees' nice to me, and friendly. God, it's a wonderful day. Goodnight!"

My heart sang. It was a brief song, and simple. And it ended with the acute consciousness that I am usually too busy to "bees" kind and friendly to my child.

Too busy to tune her in? I justify it, Lord, as preserving my own sanity. The little ones chatter so endlessly. But not to listen to them, when they are trying to tell me something, is an affront.

Too busy to accept their helpfulness? I can make cookies twice as fast alone. I can wash dishes twice as fast.

Lord, help me remember that "in a hurry" is not the way children learn things. They learn and thrive and grow when I relax and let them live at their own speed, and when I accept them as real people.

Help me, this day, to "bees" kind to them, and friendly. Help me to listen to them, and to talk to them of thy love.

Thank you, God, for the gracious prayer of a little child.

Amen.

9th Day

Dear Lord,

I come to thee to ask forgiveness for a number of things—and most of them have to do with my tongue.

Like the way I lashed out at my eldest this morning. She could not find a school book. Not such a terrible crime, really. (Goodness knows I have misplaced a thing or two myself.) But I was already irked over the spilled milk—and the squushed toothpaste—and I took it all out on her. Soundly. Unmercifully, Lord. Forgive me.

Forgive me when I say too much.

Forgive me, too, when I say nothing at all. When I do not speak to one who stands alone—and call my silence shyness. When I fail to take a stand that should be taken—and call my silence tact. When I am unwilling to witness—and tell myself, uncomfortably, that I just don't know what to say. Or that maybe this isn't a good time.

Forgive my silences, Lord.

Amen.

10th Day

Part of prayer, I have been told, is *thinking* Godward.

That is what makes it hard. I had rather *not* think. It makes me uncomfortable. I find myself turning on the radio in the car, so that the silence will be occupied and I will not find *thought* intruding upon my consciousness.

It is so much easier not to think, Lord . . . to close my mind . . . to get along with borrowed opinions and half-baked convictions. And if I catch my own mind trying to get a thought in edgewise, I need only turn up the hi-fi.

I deplore aloneness, Lord, because it confronts me with thought. And yet it may be that what I need most of all is to be alone. To be alone with thee, Lord. To think. To let the mind absorb the peace and serenity of aloneness, that it may be capable of thought, Godward. That it may be capable of prayer.

"O Lord our Lord, how excellent is thy name in all the earth!"

I lift my thought to thee.

Amen.

11th Day

Intoxicated.
That's what they were.
Those early Christians were so *caught up* with the joy, the wonder, the unbounded challenge of being part of thy divine kingdom—right there in their same old Jerusalem—that they were lifted right out of themselves.

It could happen here, Lord. That is, if we really got *caught up*.

Lord, I don't want to commit *all* of myself, *all* of my life. You know I don't want to. It would get me involved in a never-ending struggle to be the sort of person that I have committed myself to become. Never-ending struggles ask an awful lot.

And yet, Lord, I've had some brief glimpses of that heady joy, that stirring wonder that lifts me right out of myself and into thy presence. It was an intoxicating moment, Lord—and I would give anything to experience it again.
> Anything? Myself? Even *all* of myself? Even so, Lord.

Accept my fragmented self, my Father, and make me wholly thine.
Wholly, joyfully, radiantly thine.

Amen.

12th Day

Dear Lord, I'm tired this day. Bone weary.

Would you like to listen to my troubles? Only you could understand a day like this one.

I have tied innumerable shoestrings, wiped noses, arbitrated squabbles, bandaged knees, washed piles of dishes—most of which are now dirty again—scorched one white shirt, burned one pot of beans, and spilled grape Kool-aid on the kitchen floor. I have kicked the dog, snarled at the kids, and felt sorry indeed for poor little me.

Now I'm bringing the whole mess to you, Lord. Some days are just more than I can handle.

Wait a minute. There are two things wrong with what I just said. I meant, some days *I* am more than I can handle.

And then, I almost forgot that we are in this thing together—thee and me.

Be still, my soul. The Lord is on thy side.

What matter the frustrations, the dailiness, the dishes? What matter, really? Be still, my soul. Unwind. Be still.

I was weary when I came here, Father.
I rest in thee.

Amen.

13th Day

Dear Lord, I want to *want* to pray.

Will that day ever come?

I come to this time of quiet each day, dutifully. Will I arrive someday to the place of spiritual growth where I will come *eagerly*, hardly able to *wait* to enter into conversation with thee?

Lord, I want to *want* to read the Bible. I go to it occasionally, to look up something. I read it through once, years ago. But it was a hard, slow grind. And what I felt when I finished was, "Aren't I the pious one!" instead of, "Lord, I feel closer to thee."

Perhaps it is like a growing friendship. I meet a stranger, who becomes an acquaintance. If we give, and share, and seek each other out, this ripens into a friendship. And if, by some happy circumstance we have found a kindred spirit, then we look forward eagerly to each meeting.

We were one-sided strangers at first, you and I. You have known and sought me always, but I have just begun to get acquainted with you. Each day, as I set aside this time for conversation, I get to know you better, Lord.

And you created me a kindred spirit. So the possibilities for this fellowship are richly promising. I need only care enough to seek thee, seeking me.

Amen.

14th Day

It's hard to shut out the world, Lord.

I am here in this quiet place, sitting still, and waiting for that stirring of the heart that is communion with thee.

But my mind isn't still. It's racing off in all directions at once—making endless lists of things I *must* attend to, calculating the yards of gingham that would be required to make new kitchen curtains, wondering vaguely what to fix for supper.

Settle down, mind. Stop your restless wandering, for I am here to pray.

Settle down, mind. Think only, this moment, of God.
> God who is great.
> God who is good.
> God who is love.

Dear Lord, I become more aware of thee as I pray. I feel the wonder of thy nearness.

I want deeply to take this feeling with me, back into my kitchen. Lord, bless with Mary's spirit my Martha kind of life.

Amen.

15th Day

She snuggled down in bed, Lord, with her battered old teddy bear, and started her prayers.

"Dea' God," she began, for she cannot yet pronounce her "r's," "Thank you fo' this day. Thank you fo' my fwends. And thank you fo' my wa'm tuffy bed. Amen."

Amen, Lord. Thank you for this day—for roses by the window, for the barely cracked mud pie graciously presented by a solemn little boy, for the heart-lifting smile of a friend.

Thank you for the smell of rain, and for the exciting, unthinkable magic of a dipper full of stars. Thank you for this night.

Let my eyes never get so blind or so tired that they fail to see as a child sees. May the first crocus always be a delight. And the seventeenth crocus, as well.
And a ladybug.
And a leaf of grass.

Thank you, God, for all the magnificent "little" things of this day.

Amen.

16th Day

Dear Lord, there is more work to praying than I had counted on. I guess I had expected a sort of magic—whereby I could come here to this place of quiet, sit a moment in patient anticipation, and then be appropriately rewarded with a comfortable warm feeling called worship.

It is not always thus. There's more to worship than a good feeling in your insides.

So I've rolled up my sleeves, Lord, and I'm here to pray.

First, there is the ever-present problem of tuning out the world.

Lord, I come alone, to thee, to share a moment of quietness. When my mind wanders, I will fetch it back again. Strange how you can assign a task to a part of your mind—like, "Sit here and pray"—while another part hurries back to the kitchen, or the mending pile, or the weeds in the flower bed.

Here! Here I am, Lord. All of me.
    I pray for quietness of mind.
    I pray for serenity of spirit.
    I pray for depth of devotion to thee.
    To thee, I pray, to thee.

                Amen.

17th Day

Dear Lord,

do I dare try to pray the prayer of St. Francis? It gets so personal and incriminating. It asks a lot.

"Lord, make us instruments of thy peace.
Where there is hatred, let us sow love;
Where there is injury, pardon;
Where there is discord, union;
Where there is doubt, faith;
Where there is despair, hope;
Where there is darkness, light;
Where there is sadness, joy;
O Divine Master, grant that I may not so much seek
To be consoled, as to console;
To be understood, as to understand;
To be loved, as to love;
For it is in giving, that we receive;
It is in pardoning, that we are pardoned;
It is in dying, that we are born to eternal life."

Thy mind and thy spirit, Lord.
Instruments of thy peace.
Seek not so much to be loved as to love.
I will try to live this prayer.

Amen.

18th Day

Dear Lord,
there must be a better way.

I *know* there's a better way. My haphazard approach
to things is not really "casual living"—it's sloppy and
ineffective living. You know, Lord, that I can find
forty other things to do when it is time to pray—and
at the moment each one seems valid. But when something comes up that *I* want to do, I can let everything
else go without so much as a second thought.
As a result I am usually behind with my work, and
always behind in my conversations with thee. And I
feel put upon because I have so much to do in so
little time.

So, Lord, help me tidy up my thinking.
I need to get it settled about which things come first.
I need to do more than sweep away mental cobwebs.
I need to straighten and sort—file some lesser things
away, eliminate some unworthy clutter, dust off some
solid convictions.

Then I would not waste time, Father, on fuzzy and
unusable resolves, nor on vaguely good intentions.
With a mind cleared, perhaps I could grapple with
eternals.

"Take from [my] soul the strain and stress,
And let [an] ordered life confess
The beauty of thy peace."

Amen.

19th Day

"Bless the Lord, O my soul:
    and all that is within me, bless his holy name."

All that is within me.

All, Lord?

I find within me some things that do not tend to
bless thy holy name.
Self-consciousness, for instance, that wants only to
bless *my* holy name.
Bitterness, sometimes, that doesn't want to bless *anybody's* holy name.

When I stand back and look within me, Lord,
I find anxieties, petty resentments, unlovely ambitions—and everlastingly this self-firstness. These do
not bless.

Any motive or thought or attitude that puts *me* in the
center of my life, and tries to fit righteousness and
related virtues around it, ends in frustration. The
blessed life is not so constructed.

Lord, giver of my life, be also center of my life.
When I orient myself to thee, I find peace.
When I orient my motives, my attitudes, my thinking around thee,
I find myself.

"Bless the Lord, O my soul:
    and all that is within me, bless his holy name."

All that is within me.

Amen.

20th Day

Dear Lord, I don't really want to talk to you this morning.
I'm afraid.

To sit up here and mouth a bunch of sweet nothings, and call it prayer, is a waste of your time and mine, too. It must be *honest*, it must be genuine, or it isn't prayer.

This is what scares me, Lord. If I pray honestly for the strength to be a bigger person, well—maybe I will be—and maybe I won't like it at all. There might be things to give up, pet peeves to live above, private vices to eliminate. I don't know if I *want* to be all that good.

Our Father, who art in heaven, I come honestly to you in prayer, because you are my Father. No pretense needed here, Lord. It's just me, talking to you, about things as they are.

Hallowed be thy name. Holy and revered in my own heart—so that just to say "Lord" is prayer.

Thy kingdom come. Now. In me. Whatever else has to go, to make room for it. Thy kingdom of love dwell within me today—and all my tomorrows.

Amen, amen.

21st Day: A Meditation on the Twenty-Third Psalm

Lord, my shepherd,

I have no real "wants" outside of thee.
When I am with thee, all pastures are green and life-giving. It is when I stray away that even the finest grasses do not satisfy.
Thy way leads beside still waters. It is the bypaths, the sidetracks of my own choosing that lead with feverish momentum to frustration.

Thy peace restores my soul.
Replenishes. Makes whole again.
Thy way is a path of right living. There is no hidden innerself, no pretense, no sham. Only a path of righteousness wherein I walk.
I fall, sometimes. But the error is mine. The way is righteous, and I may get up and walk in it again.

Sometimes the way leads through the valley of the shadow of death. But death also is life. I need not fear, for thou art with me.
Thee—and me. Why should I need to be afraid?
And when in that valley of the shadows I mourn, I find comfort in thee, for thou art with me.

I have no enemies—all men are thy children. I seek to understand them and, understanding, to love them.

My heart is not big enough to contain the blessing of belonging to thee.

For thou art with me.
And this shall be so, all the days of my life.
        Thou art with me.

                            Amen.

22nd Day

Dear Lord,

I do not pray to a vague oblong blur.
Nor do I bring my prayers to a Grandfather-Santa-Claus type, who genially grants my momentary whim.

Lord, I pray to thee, creative Spirit who made this world, and who made every living cell within it. More, Lord, than this—for you have made *all* worlds that are, or ever will be. And if, in those other worlds there are also living cells, well, you made those, too.

Oh, the unmitigated gall of little me, that I should seek conversation with the God of interplanetary space!

But Lord, it is you who have made this conversation possible—and you who have made it necessary. You put within me a spark of divinity, a scrap of your own divine nature, that makes me feel restless and insecure—and *lonesome*—until I am with thee.

God of all worlds that are, what an incomprehensible wonder that you are even *aware* of me,
>and that you know me and love me, Lord,
>and that you seek me, even as I seek you.

Here I am, Lord, meekly kneeling upon my knees.
Here I am, Lord, keenly conscious this moment of thy majesty, and of my cosmic insignificance.
Keenly conscious also of thy love.
It is to thee I pray,
>My Father, who is in heaven,
>hallowed be thy name.

>Amen.

23rd Day

Lord, the saints of ages past all seem to agree that one element of true prayer is to ask forgiveness for our sins.

Mine are the ordinary little sins, Father.
Still, if they are to stand in the way of my communing with thee, well then I will admit them, and you will forgive them.

Nagging is the first one. I hate to even use the word. It speaks of a failing I despise in others and try to ignore in myself. But I *do* nag, Lord, and I am heartily sorry for it. When I fuss at the kids, I so often say too much, too long. When I speak to my husband, what I have to say is too often faultfinding. To nag at someone else is to take the shine off his day.

Is it a little thing to take the shine off another's day? No, Lord. Forgive this sin of mine.

And gossiping, Lord. Is it a little thing to spread an unkindness? To rob another of a good name, or of dignity? And if the tale I tell be intriguing, and if it gives me a feeling of superiority to tell it, and even if it be true, to pass on an unkind word is a sin.

I am sorry, Lord, for these unworthy ways. Please forgive my sins. My ugly little ordinary sins. Please help me rise above them, and live above them.

Amen.

24th Day

Father, bless my husband this day as he goes about his work.

Bless his hands, Lord—
    hands that earn our daily bread—
    hands that tousle our least one's head.
    Hands that mend tricycles, remove stickers, and
        soothe small ruffled feathers;
    hands that soothe me, too, when my own day
        has gone wrong.

I wonder how *his* day went?

Give him strength, Lord, when his burdens seem particularly heavy.
Give him wisdom, when his decisions seem hard to come by.
Give him compassion, when others are needing, or bitter, or unkind.
Give him joy, when the days are dreary ones.
Keep him stable and sweet, whether the tomorrows bring failure or whether they bring success.

Help me be big enough, Lord, to let him share his griefs and joys with me—
    big enough to complement his strengths,
    big enough to bolster his spirits,
    that he may be able to live up to thy expectations.

Thank you, God, for letting us share a life together.

Amen.

25th Day

Lord, I rushed to get here, and I'm a little out of breath. Let me unwind a minute, before I really begin to pray. Unwind. The tension of
    clocks and watches and jobs to be done,
    of lists and projects and errands to run,
    of ironing the dresses and mending the jeans,
    and baking (as soon as I put on the beans),
    and running the vacuum and scrubbing the floor,
    and how can I possibly do any more?

Unwind. Let the tension ease off a little.

Let a bed go unmade, if it must, that I might stand at the window and listen to the melody of a little purple finch.

Take the mending out to the lawn chair under a tree, and soak in the beauty of dappled leaf-shade, even as the needle flies.

Slow me down, Lord. Help me ease the tensions off a little. I get so busy taking care of those within my household that I forget to slow down and love them.

Unwind, taut mind. Slow down.

Father, God, love is not expressed on the run. This day I shall do what needs to be done, stopping often to share an unhurried moment of love with those around me. I shall take time for laughter, and for beauty, time for listening and loving. This day I shall have time for them, and time for thee.

Amen.

26th Day

Father,
I am not able to pray today.
My head aches; I hurt all over.
My thoughts are too fuzzy to focus on thee.

And yet, it is my time for prayer, and I am here.
It is not a very alert me, quite incapable of radiance,
but I am here.

Lord, whose will it is that all of us be strong and well,
I rest in thee.
My mind wanders.
It goes off on vague tangents, spins vaguer fancies.
My mind keeps dwelling on the physical miseries of
the moment, as though it took certain pleasure in in-
ward moaning and groaning.
Forgive my disconcerted mind, Lord.
Forgive my feverish ways. I rest in thee.

I toss and turn and fret, Lord.
I worry about little things that don't even matter.
It is not necessary.
Thy quietness can be my strength.
Thy strength can make me quiet.
I rest in thee.

Amen.

27th Day

If I had my druthers, Lord, I think I'd ask for patience.
I seem to need inordinate quantities. And my own natural supply runs too short, too soon.

The least ones require it—when they are learning to hold a spoon right, or tie a shoe tight.

The bigger ones require more of it, when they forget such simple every-single-day things.

Then the ones on-the-road-to-becoming—well, they need it most of all.

Like last night. How strained the situation got when our eldest was so upset, yelling his head off about trifles. And I fussed and yelled right back. Then I got enough perspective to see a little clearer, enough patience to sit down and find out what the problem really was. For once I acted as a parent, and not as another child.

Here is a new day, Lord, and I am bound to need patience before it is over.
> Patience with my husband.
> With my kids.
> Patience with my neighbors,
> and with their kids, too.

So if I had my druthers, Lord, I'd ask for patience.

Help me to walk with thee closely enough that I can reflect thy patience,
thy understanding, loving-to-infinity patience.

Amen.

28th Day

It is dismal and gray outside, Lord.
It is dismal and gray inside, too.
I have a dreary mind, today.
All I can drag from it are dull, gray, lifeless thoughts,
and sterile prayers.

No good comes from a dreary mind, Lord.

I will be honest with myself. (With thee, I have no
choice but to be honest. What is there I could hide
from thee?)

I will be honest: some days I *enjoy* being dismal.
I find a certain satisfaction in wallowing in my own
misery.
> Poor little me, Lord.
> Poor, dismal, gray little me.

A certain satisfaction.
But it isn't an *abiding* satisfaction.
And no good comes from a dreary mind.

So I will lift my thoughts up out of the dismal fog
> to thee,
> to radiance.
To a creative, living Lord, who loves even me.
Who understands me when I grovel around in my
misery,
who challenges me to look up—and laugh—and love—
and lift!

Amen.

29th Day: A Meditation on
I Corinthians 13

Lord, I am no orator, and eloquence just isn't in me. I cannot sway others with a stirring speech.

But I can love.

Lord, I am no sage. I am not even a good counselor. I don't have the ability to see through today's problems to tomorrow's solutions.

But I can love.

Lord, I haven't enough faith to take on a job like moving mountains.

But I can love.

I am not saint enough to give my life, nor even all that I possess to feed the hungry.

But I can love.

To love, really, is all that you have asked me to do.

What is it, to love?

It is to be patient, and kind, and humble.

It is to be gracious, and generous, and gentle.

It is to bear another's burdens,

to believe in his ultimate goodness,

to hope his highest hopes with him,

and to understand.

My vision is clouded. There is much that I do not understand. My thinking is hazy. Someday I shall both see and understand.

As for now, I can love.

I can love.

Amen.

30th Day

Well, the floor is mopped, Lord.
At the moment I'm too tired to enjoy it!
Housework can be such a chore.

Do you suppose it would make any difference, Lord,
if I considered it a "calling" instead?

"Called," of thee—not to mop floors, exactly, but to
make of these four walls and this roof, a home. To
make of this house a haven.

"Called," of thee—to be teacher, comforter, and
sounding board to these, my children.

"Called," of thee—to counsel with them, to discipline them, to guide them toward worthy lives of
their own. Not to dominate them; Lord, forbid. Not to
mold them into concepts of my own. But to provide for
them a climate for growth.

"Called," of thee—to be partner to my husband,
to understand and help him, to add the weight of
my shoulder to his on the wheel, thus strengthening
us both.

"Called," of thee—all of us—to make of our family a fellowship, and to make of our home a workshop
in Christian living.

Amen.

31st Day

Lord, can it be?
        How can it be?
Thy Holy Spirit dwells in me.

Has it been there all this time?
And I have been too blind to see,
too dense to know, to feel, to sense
this love within me that is thee?

How *could* I know? How *could* I see?
I'm just an underling, my Lord.
I'm just an ordinary soul.
Why should you put divinity
within the mortal likes of me?

How could I *not* know! When I love,
it is response to greater love.
When I seek thee honestly, I see
thou art already seeking me.
And Father, when I pray,
I sense thyself in what I say.

Thy Holy Spirit dwells in me.
So let me live, my Lord, this day.

                        Amen.

MY SPECIAL DAYS
AND SEASONS

January

Well, Lord, we have come again to the two-faced month of Janus.

The old Romans, who did not know you, must have had some glimpse of truth when they gave their god Janus two faces—one for looking backward, the other for looking ahead.

Lord, when you look back on my year just finished, you see a lot of things *un*finished—

> dreams I had, and didn't do,
> plans that I did not pursue;
> projects started, set aside;
> promises to thee—denied.

Lord, if I had just *carried through* more of the kindnesses that I *thought* about doing—well, it would have been a better year.

But you look forward, too, and so shall I. Here lies a whole, new, fresh, uncluttered year. I shall try to put into each day of it some kindness carried through, some outside-of-myself gesture. When I see one in need of friendly words, I'll say them. When I remember another in need of a letter from me, I'll write it. When I notice a member of my household meriting praise, I'll give it.

You gave me eyes to see, Lord, and hands to do with, and a whole new year to do in. Thank you.

And let me not forget.

Amen.

February

Lord, the Cherokees called it "Hunger Moon."

And Jesus said, "Blessed are they which do hunger and thirst after righteousness: for they shall be filled."

I hunger, Lord. Not for fried chicken or strawberry shortcake—those hungers are easily satisfied.

I hunger with a restlessness, a longing for thee. Sometimes I pray, Lord—and pray—and still I am alone. I try to shut the world out, so that I may be with thee, and I find myself only with me.

I know that prayer is like this, sometimes. Communion is not automatic. You are never far away, but sometimes I am just not tuned in. Lord, I hunger for fellowship with thee. I shall keep praying. You know that I am seeking, in my own blind, groping, inept way. And I know that you are with me. Even when I do not feel your presence.

> I seek thee, Lord, knowing that you seek me.
> Knowing that I find no rest until I rest in thee.
> Knowing that this hunger, this longing, is *of* Thee, and *for* thee.
> Knowing that as surely as I seek, I will find divine fellowship.

Amen.

February 14

Was St. Valentine really a saint, Lord?
What *is* a saint, anyhow?
Outward piety is not enough. Not everyone who saith
    to thee, "Lord, Lord. . . ."
Prayer every night doesn't make a saint.
Neither does going to church every Sunday, nor read-
ing King James's own version clear through.
These are all too easy, too pat.

So *what*, Lord? What makes saints?
Sainthood is sort of like happiness.
It is not something to go out and *hunt* for, because
the harder we seek, the more unfindable it becomes.
It's a by-product.
        But a by-product of what, Lord?
        Of godly living?
        Of faithful service?
No—both are important—neither is quite enough.
Perhaps it is a by-product of love.

"Why were the saints saints?
Because they were cheerful when it was difficult to
be cheerful, patient when it was difficult to be patient,
and because they pushed on when they wanted to
stand still,
and kept silent when they wanted to talk,
and were agreeable when they wanted to be dis-
agreeable.
That was all.
It was quite simple, and always will be."

Pardon my pettiness, Lord, but what you ask is hard,
hard, hard. I will try. And I will fail.
        But thou art with me, Lord, and I must try.

Amen.

March

March came in like a lion, Lord. Like I do, some days.

> I storm and glower, and huff and puff—
> Lots of bluster and blow and bluff,
> Lots of snarl at those I love,
> Iron hand *sans* velvet glove.
>
> And then, next day, like March's lamb,
> It's aimless and witless and weak I am.
> No discipline, no rules, no aim—
> Can the lion and lamb both be the same?
>
> Can one become two? And if I do,
> Does it keep the children guessing who,
> "Is Mom a lion today? Or lamb?"
> Oh Lord, I don't know *what* I am.
>
> I only know that I'd like to be
> A stable, responsible rational "me."

So, Lord, I come to you in prayer.

I pray for stability, for strength, for a steadfast faith that is the foundation for a steadfast life.

I orient myself in thee, so that I need not flutter with the prevailing winds, but rather stand firm with a prevailing faith.

Thou art my rock and my fortress.

Thou art my strength.

Amen.

I sing as I arise today.

Not right away, Lord. Not when I first got up.
But now I sing! Breakfast is attended to,
my husband and the scholars are off.
The beds are made, the sun is shining in my kitchen
window, and I sing!

I sing as I arise today.
I call upon the Father's might,
The will of God to be my guide,
The eye of God to be my sight.

O Lord, that I might see through thy all-seeing eyes.
That I might see this day the loneliness of those who
are alone, the heartache of those who mourn,
the yearning of those who seek thee, and do not *know*
they seek thee.
I pray this day that I might see, like thee.

The Word of God to be my speech,

that I might say this day the right, the helpful, the
God-given word.

The hand of God to be my stay,
The shield of God to be my strength
The path of God to be my way.

The path of God. O Lord, I pray
I may not wander off today,
but walk, with seeing eyes, the way,
and speak the words you'd have me say,
And sing—thy song!

I sing as I arise today.

Amen.

April

Sometimes I *do* understand, Lord.

How could anyone look deep into the heart of a tulip
and *not* believe? The beauty, the perfection, the ma-
jestic dignity of just one bloom could not be a botanical
accident.
You made it, Lord, and just looking at it is a benedic-
tion.

I planted the bulbs, Lord. I watered and weeded the
flower bed. Does that make us partners? You put the
promise of life into those dull, dry bulbs. I could not
do that. Neither could Carver, nor Burbank, nor anyone else. But Lord, *you needed my help.* Somebody
had to plant and water and weed.

Partners. Is that what it means—
"partakers of the divine nature"?

Partners with thee. The idea is too big for me, Lord.
It sets my brain reeling. If I could be willing to turn
myself over to thee, *entirely,* what might we be able
to do for the kingdom, together!

Lord, I believe—help thou my unbelief!

Amen.

April 15

I have been thinking about money, Lord.
This is the time of year for that sort of thinking.
And I have been thinking about the lack of it, too.
Seems like the supply is always insufficient.
Insufficient for what, though?
For the necessities?

> No—my house is roofed and warm.
> My children are clothed and fed.

(I can talk to you about sunsets and purple finches,
Lord—but I get uncomfortable talking about money.
Could that be incriminating?)
Lord, *stewardship* involves all of life.
But it involves money, too.
It requires an awareness of what I am spending,
    and what I am spending it for.
It requires an examination of *wants*.
It requires a consciousness and study of the needs of
    thy children.

What do I really want?
I know we enjoy our own warm house and pot roast
so much more if we have shared it.
But the bills aren't paid. And that is a nagging burden.
Lord, forgive. It is an excuse, too.
Keeping up with the Joneses is a luxury I cannot afford.
But sharing the burden of another family's leaking
roof and empty larder is a responsibility I cannot
evade.
Money means nothing, except for what it can buy.
Let me spend mine for things that matter.

Amen.

May

It's May already, Lord, and school will soon be out. For the kids, that is.

Not for me. I haven't learned enough. "School" better stay in session a long time yet for me.

Lord, I am beginning to realize that *learning* is a verb of the present tense—almost never of the past. And *knowledge* doesn't come with a period after it. Just about the time I think I *know* something, I glimpse whole new facets to the matter. The more I learn, the more aware I become of how much there is yet to learn.

I may never *know* a great deal, Lord, but keep me learning. I shall never arrive, but keep me seeking. You gave me a mind. I have contented myself with using only a part of it. Now I am ready for some mental calisthenics. I want to learn!

Let's see—I can read. And thank you, God, for the thinkers of all the ages who have taken the time to write down some of their discoveries, for me.

I can listen. I could learn something from every person I know. How to tell a starling from a shrike. How to make a better apple pie. Why committees tick. How to prune a rose. I can learn by listening.

I can pray, Lord. This time of quiet is my spiritual school. I shall not graduate from it. But, in thy presence, I shall grow in wisdom, and in knowledge, and in fellowship with thee.

Amen.

Mother's Day

It is only a house, Lord—with walls, and a front door,
with a back screen that nearly always slams,
and a roof over our heads.
Only a house—wood, and shingles, and affection, and
concern, and family jokes. Mortar and bricks, and
laughter, and heartache, and radiant joy.

It's a home.
God, bless our home.
And God, help me make it all the things it has got
to be.

A *haven,* when we need it. A place of comfort, where
we can get over the bruising things that happen.
A *school,* where all of us can learn how to cope with
ourselves, and with other selves as well.
A *church!* Yes, Lord, a segment of the fellowship
of believers. A place of worship, a place for finding
out what God is like.
A *launching platform,* when the young 'uns are old
enough to go out into orbits of their own. And for all
of us—for when we are comforted, and taught, and
inspired, we need to launch out, too.

The *good* of the world is home-spawned, Lord.
All I need to do is make my home the sort of place
where these things happen.

Father, God, I need your help.

Amen.

June

June is for brides, Lord. For new brides, bless 'em—and for us brides of other Junes as well.

Father, thank you for marriage—and especially for mine. It is not just what I thought it was going to be. That starched fresh apron I was going to wear doesn't stay very starched when a three-year-old wipes his grubby paws on it, or when a six-year-old sneaks it out for playing Superman. But it is my symbol of domesticity, and I love it.

Books for June brides talk about candlelight and romance. But there ought to be a first chapter called "Married Life Is Family Life." I had not really thought about *that*, Lord—not when I was a June bride. But when the children that we wanted *came*, it was scared young me who had the dreadful and holy and wonderful and awful responsibility of their character.

Lord, not all marriages—not *any* marriages—turn out to be quite like the first June dreams. But working at it, struggling to make a *real* home, losing my life in my family, putting into my marriage the very best that I can—this is my challenge and my salvation. Father, help me.

Bless the brides of this June, Lord. And bless this bride of a June past. Let me count among my blessings the remembered dreams, the starched aprons, the grubby fingers, and the bologna sandwiches.

And gird me with the strength I am going to need to cope with the tomorrows.

Amen.

July

Lord, Father,
> My body is here in prayer.
> My mind is, too, sort of.

But it's hot today. My thoughts are limp and frazzled.
All wilted into a lethargic little puddle.

It's good corn weather, though. Thank you, Father, for hot summer days when corn grows tall and lush and green. Thank you for hot summer days when my children play in the sprinkler and loll in the shade, their own growing unhampered by the scheduled restrictions of other times of year.

Thank you, Lord, for hot summer days, when the pace is a little slower and the living more relaxed. I shall not let them melt into lazy do-nothing days. I shall try to make them growing days for all of us.

Lord, you have given us a world of beauty and wonder—a world of tall corn, of ladybugs, and the dappled shade of a tree. Let me see it. Let me *see* the beauty of a leaf of grass, the miracle of every little creature, "miracle enough to stagger sextillions of infidels."

Lord, you have given us a world of growth. Those living things which open themselves to thy sun, and soak up thy rain, and bask in the summer heat—those things grow, and flourish.

> I want to grow, too, Lord.
> I want to grow tall,
> > and vital,
> > and alive.

Amen.

July 4

Lord, I thank you for the privilege of living in this, my country. It is not perfect, nor always just, nor always right. But it is a nation founded on freedom and striving for justice. I am glad, and grateful, that I am an American.

Seems that I have some responsibility here, too, Lord. Being "only a housewife" does not exonerate me. Being a citizen implicates me. On voting day, best I be there, and be informed. When discussion comes up, best I take a stand for what I believe to be right, and just, and godly. Even when I'd rather not. Maybe I have more time than anyone else in my family, really, to study the issues. Maybe I have more influence than I realize. Everyone does, I guess. Like the pebble tossed in the pond.

Influence for what? For justice? Yes, and for honor, and uprightness. And for thee.

"In God we trust," it says. Do we? Do I?
"One nation under God," it says. Are we?
Am I?

The highest allegiance, as a person and as a people, is to thee.

> "Our father's God, to Thee,
> Author of liberty,
> To Thee we sing:
> Long may our land be bright
> With freedom's holy light;
> Protect us by Thy might,
> Great God, our King."

Amen.

August

It's unthinkable, Lord.
Especially in August.
The stars have a quality of beauty that is not theirs
on other nights. The brightness of them, and the vast-
ness of the spaces in between—well, it's unthinkable.
I just can't think *big* enough to take it all in.

But "when I consider thy heavens, the work of thy
fingers, the moon and the stars, which thou hast
ordained . . ." especially on an August night—
then I remember that the Lord of the universe is
Lord of me, too.

Tonight I shall not do any useful, mundane thing,
like darning socks, or letting out hems, or beginning
the cross-stitching of a Christmas apron.

Tonight I shall spread Grandma's old quilt on the
grass. There I shall sit, and take a long deep breath
of roses, honeysuckle, and August night. I shall open
my ears to the drowsing sparrows and the raucous
cicadas, and perhaps, with luck, to the song of a frog.

All day long I have gone around in the maddening
circles of what's for lunch, and is it time to pick up
the girls at the pool, and I've just got to clean out
the cabinet under the kitchen sink, if I can get the
floor mopped in time. All day—maddening circles.

But now it is an August night. I need its peace for
restoring my soul. I need its blessed in-betweenness
for recharging my batteries.
I sit in the evening cool, and find Cassiopeiae and the
Big Dipper, and let the unthinkable heavens declare
to me thy glory, and thy love.

Amen.

September

Well, I got them off to school, Lord.

There is something about the sight of a tablet and pencil, the smell of a new box of crayons, that makes me covet that thrill of learning I had when *my* first tablet was new.

It has been a long time since I really *set* myself to learning something new. And yet this mind you gave me, Lord, is capable of tasks far beyond those I give it. Capable of grasping things more vital than the price of eggs this week, and how much milk has gone up. Capable of wrestling with new truths—of comprehending, even in small ways, the magnitude of space, the multitude of ideas, the beatitude of grace.

My mind needs stretching, Lord. My thinking has become bound. It does not often reach beyond the four walls of my house. I have thought so long on the level of a preschooler that I may have forgotten how to think big. I want to learn.

But it is not automatic. The prerequisite is study, and that takes effort. I may forget these noble ideas by tomorrow. But right now, in this moment, I know that challenging my mind is responding to thee.

So, Lord, this day I shall *read*—something new, and hard, and stimulating. This day I shall *think*—no flitting wisp of a thought, mind you; I shall ponder. This day I shall *learn.*

My child and I are starting back to school, Lord. May we never let a day go by without learning something new.

Never let a day go by.

Amen.

October

Thank you, Lord, for Indian summer!

I don't know why we call it that. Maybe the Indians took time to enjoy it, time to drink it in, time to savor these summer-is-gone-but-winter-is-not-yet-here days.

I thought winter *had* come, Lord. I got the coats out, and found the mittens. Now, suddenly, the days are warmer. The mornings have a crisp delight that sets them apart—and only the evenings have the chilly reminder that this is a brief respite.

Why, Lord? Why Indian summer?
Are these special gift-days from thee, as the Indians said they were? Are they another chance to gather in the harvest of the fall? Are they a time for storing up beauty and warmth and peace?

If these *are* special gift-from-God days, I should do something special with them.
For one thing, I shall enjoy them.
 I shall look with eyes that see
 at the dazzle of the sun,
 at the blue-smoke haze of the sky—
 at the burnished gold of the sycamore leaves in
 my neighbor's yard.
I shall store up in my soul
 as much of the color of ivy and chrysanthemum,
 as much of the beauty of cloud pattern and harvest moon,
 as much of Indian summer as I can contain.

Then, Lord, when winter comes, and cold winds whistle outside my door,
I can bask again in these gift-days of October.

Amen.

November

Our Father, you have given us this day our daily bread.
The grain is ripe. Some fields are cut, and the strong, good smell of earth hovers over them. Harvest is not far away.

It may not be a bumper crop this year. Even so, we have our daily bread. For this, I give thanks.

For daily bread. For the cotton cloth on my kitchen table, and the sun coming in the window. And for the burnished sheen on that apple I polished.

It may not be a magazine-cover kitchen, Lord. The stove is old, but it still bakes good bread. *Daily* bread. There is a peace here in my kitchen, a sunniness that is more than that which comes through the window.

The table may not be glamorously spread for supper tonight, Lord. But there will be savory stew. There will be homemade jelly. And there will be bread. Daily bread. This, with thee, is enough.

> I give thanks.
> My cup runneth over.

> Amen.

Thanksgiving

"On the first Thanksgiving, long, long ago,
The little children stood in a row
By the loaded table of rough new wood
And thanked the Lord for all things good.

"Jonathon whispered a little prayer
Thanking God for the crisp, fall air,
For turkey and deer he had learned to shoot,
For good sweet corn, and the red beet root,
For a log house home in a strange new land,
For a brave and humble pilgrim band.

"Little Patience started to say
'Thank you, God, for a happy day. . .'
And then she added, 'Thank you, too,
For my corn-husk doll in calico blue,
For my friend Small Dove with the black, black hair,
And for your wise and loving care.'"

On this Thanksgiving, we gather to pray
Our prayer of thanks on a special day,
Around a table, simply spread,
With good potroast, and homemade bread.

We thank you for harvest, nearly done,
For the blessed rain and the blessed sun.
For each one here, the grown, the small—
And for thy Love, which seeks us all.

Amen.

December

"I would not deny him
  Any gaieties
  Of Santa Claus and reindeer
  And wonder-laden trees;

But let a song ring clearly
  And let a star shine through,
  And when he thinks of Christmas, Lord,
  Let him think of You."

Dear Lord, let these days before Christmas be full of wonder and joy in this house. I am getting in a dither again—but let me remember that the *nicest* gift I can give my children is Christmas itself. Give me the patience to help them *make* presents; the restraint to let them wrap them, all by themselves. Let me love enough to invite small hands to participate in the ritual of Christmas cookies. Let me find time to help them remember others, whose Christmas may be scant this year.

Father, a birthday is childhood's big event. Help me teach my children what *this* birthday is all about. I cannot *tell* them *how* love came down at Christmas. Help me *show* them.

And when they think of Christmas, Lord,
  let them think of you.

Amen, amen.

Christmas Day

The setting was so simple, Lord.
A sheltered place, where animals were stabled.
The earthy smell of the creatures, and of the hay.
The soft light of a burning wick in a clay vessel,
   and the warmth of a little fire.
The sounds of Joseph's donkey, munching hay—
   a mouse, scurrying in the straw.
Into such a setting the Christ was born.

And shepherds came.
Came because you called them, Lord—
     to come and see—
     to see and marvel,
     and to kneel.
I come, too, Lord. Because you call me to come.
The angel song I hear is within.
But if I listen, I hear it clearly.
     I marvel.
     I kneel.
"What is man, that thou art mindful of him?
and the son of man, that thou visitest him?"

Wise men came. Sages. Kings, perhaps.
Why did *they* come?
     Because you called them, Lord?
     To come and see—
     to see and marvel,
      and to kneel.
I come, too, Lord. Because you call me to come.
The star I see is somewhere behind my eyes.
But the star is thine, and I come.
     I marvel.
     I kneel.
"Bless the Lord, O my soul: and all that is within me,
bless his holy name."

                Amen.

December 26

And the wise men came bringing gifts.

It had been a long journey, I suppose. A journey of faith, with no road maps. A journey of love, too, Lord.

Ah, so. We all make our journey of faith—and of love—in search of thee. We all, if we are willing to undertake the journey, make certain decisions. Some things we must turn our backs on. Some things we must leave behind. But the hardest part is *believing* enough to start off—with no road map.

Lord, it is thee I seek. Others who have found a vital and *real* fellowship with thee have left a few words of wisdom. But no road map. I must find my own way to thee.

I keep stopping by the wayside to attend to lesser things. I keep getting sidetracked. Still, the star challenges, and I start off again on my blundering, searching way.

It *is* a journey of love. I search because of thy love, reaching out to me. I search because of that love within me, reaching out to thee.

And when the wise men found thee, in the place where a young child lay, they worshiped.

Ah, so, Lord. And even as I journey, thou art with me.

Amen.

December 27

I keep thinking about those wise men, Lord.
They brought gifts.
But thy son, the Christ, is no longer a baby in a manger.
I cannot make a pilgrimage to Bethlehem with Persian magi—nor even with Palestinian shepherds.
So what is this about gifts to me?

I am here and now.
The gifts I bring to thee must be given to thy children.
That sounds too easy, Lord. Everybody loves to give presents.
I do it for my family, for a few special friends.
That is not what you meant, is it, Lord?
Or at least that's not all of it.

"For if ye love them which love you, . . . what do ye more than others?"

A gift to thee.

Does that mean I should go out in search of one in need, and then minister to him in thy name? Or would that make me a prying, nosey do-gooder?

Does it mean an everyday attitude of sharing that just *naturally* sees needs, and as naturally gives? What about me? I'm naturally sort of blind.

Is it a search of one who shall receive? Is it an awareness?

Or am I just making the whole thing complicated, Lord, when it is really so simple:

> I cannot *give* what I do not have.
> No gift is worthy, except love.
> I can't give it if I don't have it.
> And *with* love, all gifts are to thee.

Amen.

Communion Sunday

Lord, I come now to this quiet place to repeat the prayer we said in church this Communion day. I felt then the need of praying it over, more slowly, more personally.

Almighty God, creator of all that I know and love,
  my Father and my Lord,
*unto whom all hearts are open, all desires known,
and from whom no secrets are hid*—no secrets, Lord.
You know the unworthy motives, the unkind attitudes.
and all the little secret faults. You know, Lord.
*Cleanse the thoughts of my heart
by the inspiration of Thy Holy Spirit*—that part of thy
divine nature that dwells in me, Lord. Let it motivate,
and challenge, and fill the thoughts of my heart.
That I may perfectly love Thee—
  without reservation,
  without exception,
  without exclusion—
  just love thee, with all my heart and mind and
soul and strength, *that I may worthily magnify Thy
holy Name.*

Amen.

Birthday

This is my birthday, Lord, and I thank you for the years and the days that have been mine. I've spent some of them grumbling, goodness knows. I don't remember now just what it was that I grumbled about. Little things, I suppose, like "Hamburger for supper *again!*" and *"Why* can't they learn to pick up their own things?" Or else I have grumbled over imagined hurts, like "Nobody understands me," or "I'm just not appreciated."

Mostly, though, these have been good years. Instead of birthdays I will count blessings—my childhood—the glorious joys of those awkward growing-up years (and the very fact that I survived the abysmal sorrows) —the friends who have so enriched my living—my husband—my children—work to do, and strength of body and mind for the doing of it. For these things I thank you.

This is my birthday, Lord. It may be that I will have as many years ahead as I have behind me this day. But I am not immortal. Those things that I was going to do with my life, I'd best get on with.

I'd best get on with them, Lord.
I do not know what the tomorrows hold,
but I do know that you hold the tomorrows.
For this I thank you.

Amen.

Moving Day

Moving is a headache, Lord—
>and a backache.
>And a pain in the neck.

But the time comes—
and the family accumulations are there to be packed,
or discarded, and there is nothing to do but get with it.

I need to do some spiritual sorting and packing, too,
Lord. There are things I ought to leave behind.

Prejudice, for one. My uneasy awareness of the irrelevant things that separate us.

Busyness. This is a good time to stop and take stock before I join a burdening abundance of organizations and good causes.

Fears. There really isn't room to pack them, and I certainly don't need them.

Maybe I ought to leave my *reputation* behind, lest I be resting on dry laurels, or nursing old failures.

This is a new start, Lord. A new life, almost.

Let me take with me anticipation—
>a fresh outlook,
>and a clean slate.

Let me begin again,
>building on what I have that is worth taking along,
>open-eyed, and adventuring for thee.

>Amen.

A Day of Birth

"For unto us a child is born"
unto us a life is given,
and its development shall be upon our shoulders.

This is a high and holy time, Lord,
this day of birth.
I have been part of a miracle.
The life which for these last months has stirred within
me lives now on its own.

Such tiny fingers, and yet so perfect.
Such ridiculously small little toes.
Hair as soft as down.
Ears so intricately designed.
Eyes that regard me with wise, unseeing stare.

It is a miracle, Lord.
This tiny perfect body has come from the union of two
cells.
Nobody but you could have thought of a miracle like
this.
It is a miracle, and I have been part of it.

The growing up, the person that this tiny child is to become—well, that's a sort of miracle, too.
And I will be part of that.

Father, lead me. It is wisdom I need.
The deep, understanding wisdom that guides a little
child in a strange new world.
Father, lead me.

Amen.

A Day of Death

It never seemed *real* before, Lord.

Death doesn't, I guess, until it happens to someone very near.

Before, it had been something that happens only to other people.

Now it has happened to us.

And even when we knew that it must come, it was so sudden . . . and so final.

And it hurts, Lord. Aloneness is a pain. Absence is an empty ache. How can I stand it, Lord? How can I live with this loss?

He was so little.

And he had a hold upon our hearts that will never let us go.

I am being selfish, I suppose.

The hurting makes it hard to see from his point of view. He has gone home—to thee. Isn't that what we said we wanted?

To be with thee? And now he is.

Father, God. Help me keep my perspective.

I shall miss him so—the touch of his grubby little hand —the lilt of his voice—

how many times will I turn to speak to him, or set his place at the table, and remember anew that he is not here?

I try to remember, Lord. I try to rejoice.

I do not understand it, but I can accept it.

I have known your goodness and your love all my life.

You have led me this far, lead me on.

You do not forsake him now.

Neither do you forsake us, who walk for a while through the valley of the shadows.

Amen.

Reflection

Lord, this one thing I can now accept:
> I cannot undo death.

It is not death that I need to undo. It is the attitudes
that I have had toward it. Death is natural. It is as
much a part of living as life.

Lord, I am trying to grasp the meaning of this, and
my hurting gets in the way.

This has not been thy will—this one death that has
come to us. You have not sent it to chasten, nor even
to strengthen us.

You have not *sent* it. Death is so often a result of
man's inadequacies.

But dear God, it *is* thy will that we should come
through such an experience stronger—bigger—and
somehow closer to thee.

What is it you are saying to us?
That we are thine?
That thou art with us—in life, in death,
> in our lives here and now after his death,
> and in his new life with thee?

Closer to thee.
Keep us so, Lord.
Let us be able to hold on to this feeling of closeness
to thee.

Now, while my heart is still tender, speak to me, Lord.
Use me. Perhaps, right now, I can see hurts and
> need and anguish that I could not see before. Use
> me, Lord.

"Blessed are they that mourn: for they shall be comforted."

Amen.

Sunday Morning

I have just come from church, Lord.
No—that isn't quite right, for we *are* the church.
I have just come from the gathered fellowship. There,
with others who also seek thee, I worshiped. There
I found comfort.
I found understanding, and a oneness of spirit within
the community of believers.
There I found thee.

Within that building, Lord, was a segment of the
gathered church. I wished that I might have stayed
there.

But if we had stayed, we who gathered there to pray,
we would have lost our high moment. It would have
become a commonplace, a mundane thing. We could
not continue to receive, with no outpouring. We
would have floundered in a degenerate and unholy
piety.

So—we left the building, and became the scattered
church.
We left because you sent us out.
We who had worshiped together were commissioned
of thee,
    to go forth, into our own neighborhoods,
    to proclaim, to the folks we see every day—
    to be the scattered fellowship,
    the church in action.

Go with us, Lord.

                Amen.

A Holy Weekday

It is a weekday, Lord,
and thy church is quiet.

Quiet. And holy.
It always seems like this when I come alone.
    The sunlight through the windows.
    The altar.

I am *confronted* with thee.

Sometimes, Lord, you speak to me,
    and I turn a deaf ear,
    and go right on pruning the rose bush.
Sometimes, Lord, you speak to me,
    and I turn my back, and walk away.

But here,
    here in thy church,
    alone, on this holy weekday,
    I am *confronted* with thee.

Deafness of ear is no defense, for nothing has been
    said.
Turning away is no solution, for I cannot.
There is a magnetism here which holds me.
I am confronted with thee.

      "Know ye that the Lord he is God:
      it is he that hath made us, and not we ourselves;
      we are his people, and the sheep of his pasture.
      Enter into his gates with thanksgiving,
      and into his courts with praise:
      be thankful unto him, and bless his name."

               Amen.

Palm Sunday

It is Palm Sunday, Lord, and I am part of the crowd.
Spectator, participant.
Not in Jerusalem, two thousand years ago.
But now—still spectator, still participant.

"And the multitudes that went before and that fol-
lowed, cried, saying, Hosanna to the son of David:
Blessed is he that cometh in the name of the Lord;
Hosanna in the highest."

God, our Father, we rejoice this day that thy Son did
come.
We rejoice.
From somewhere deep within comes a surging, mov-
ing joy
    that Christ is here.
    That he is thy Son.
    That he came in the name of the Lord, his Father
        and ours, to show us a new and better way.
Praise is not easy to say, Lord, but I feel it within.
Who needs words, when the heart rejoices?
        Hosanna!

And yet, as I sing within,
I remember with disquiet the inconstancy of
    spectators, and of participants.
I, too, who sing Hosanna, cry Crucify.
Lord, forgive, forgive.

        Amen.

Maundy Thursday

"This do in remembrance of me."

We take Communion, Lord—and I nibble my scrap
of unleavened bread, and drink my portion of the
juice of the grape—but not in remembrance of thee.
Only in uneasy consciousness that I ought to be
worshiping, and am not.

So now—later—I come to thee, to remember, and to
worship.

I do not understand all that Communion means, Lord.
I know it can be a holy moment of nearness to thee—
    a moment of newly cherished forgiveness,
    a moment of renewed dedication.
I don't suppose those who shared with him that *first*
    Communion understood, either.
But they were aware of depth, and splendor, of sor-
    row, and unconquerable joy.

And when they had shared the cup, and shared the
loaf, they sang a hymn, and went out into the night.

What a way to face night, Lord!
What a strength and a shield—
to face whatever the night may hold for us with a joy,
    a triumphant joy in the heart,
and a hymn of praise—a stirring, undergirding hymn
of praise.

So—a Communion shared, and a hymn.

                Amen.

Good Friday

Why *good*, Lord?
This was the day the inconstant participants cried,
"Crucify!"
This was the day they nailed thy Son to a cross,
and laid him in a borrowed tomb.

Why *good*? I don't know, Lord, I don't know.
Because it had to be?
Because the depths of Friday had to be experienced
before the triumphant joy of Easter could be possible?
Because of a cup? A cup which thy Son chose to take
up and to drink?

Because *I* had to have a sign?
This was real drama, unfolding before the Passover
crowd.
He didn't *have* to die—he *chose* to die.

For me? To give me a sign?
To show us all, spectators and participants,
the lows to which man will stoop—
the highs to which God-in-man can rise?
To show us what redemption really means?

"O Love divine, what hast Thou done!
Th' incarnate God hath died for me! . . .
Is crucified for me and you,
To bring us rebels back to God."

I rebel, Lord. I rebel against more theology that I
can understand.
I rebel against more discipline than I can enjoy.
I rebel against more surrender that I want to give.
I rebel against thee, Lord.

Father, forgive, and bring us rebels back to thee.

Amen.

Easter Sunday

Lord, I make no pretense of understanding the miracle
of Resurrection.
But something happened.
Something unbelievable, and undeniable.
It happened to Peter and John—to Mary and Martha
and Johanna.

And, Lord, it happened as surely to me.

I do not know where the *surety* comes from, other
than that it comes from thee.
And when I see Easter lilies, or apple blossoms, and
when I hear the Hallelujahs,
something wells up within me,
something tremendous, and uncontainable.
And I know!

I know because of the unreasoned joy,
because of this inner response to thy love,
    that life is only a beginning—
    that it shall endless be!
        Hallelujah.

                Amen.

Pentecost

And they all felt the presence of the Spirit of God.

They must have, Lord.
It must have been a mighty moment, to make a huddled group of disillusioned fishermen and other humble folk go out and turn the world upside down.

What I sometimes feel is a heart-warming awareness
—but not a soul-shaking mighty moment.
Not Pentecost!

Why, Lord?
>Because I don't *look* for it?
>Because I don't *want* it to happen?
To them, yes.
But not to me.
It might shake the *status quo*.
Warmness of heart, yes, Lord.
But tongues of flame? Please, no.

And yet—
>and yet there is a longing in me to give all of myself, *without reservation*, to something worthy, something big.
There is a longing within me for tongues of flame.
For Pentecost.

>Spirit of the Living God,
>Fall afresh on me.
>Spirit of the Living God,
>Fall afresh on me.
>Melt me,
>Mold me,
>Fill me,
>Use me.
>Spirit of the Living God,
>Fall afresh on me.

>>Amen.

MY ORDINARY DAYS

For all the saints, Lord,
for all the endless line of splendor,
for those great souls seeking thee,
whose very search makes mine surer,
for the *famous* saints, I'm grateful, Lord.
I forget about them. They lived, and stood staunchly
for thee, and died—all so long ago.
And yet, this very time of prayer is part of the rich
heritage they left to me.
Thank you, Lord, for the stalwart saints of the ages.

Thank you, too, for the saints of *this* day—the lesser
saints.
The ones I know.
The ones with whom I have walked and talked.
Thank you, God our Father, for my family, from
whom I first learned of thee.
And thank you for those outside the circle of family
who cared enough,
and shared enough, to point me on toward thee.
They, too, are saints.
There are other saints, Lord—sometimes I never even
know their names,
whose lives I simply glimpse in passing,
but whose special radiance is thine.
Thank you for these saints, too.
Thank you for the ages-long and endless line of
splendor.

> "Praise God, from whom all blessings flow;
> Praise Him, all creatures here below,
> Praise him above, ye heavenly host:
> Praise Father, Son, and Holy Ghost."

> Amen, amen.

They just flew over, Lord.
A long, ever-changing, never-changing "V" of geese,
headed due north. How do they know North?

> "He who, from zone to zone,
> Guides through the boundless sky [their]
> certain flight,
> In the long way that I must tread alone,
> Will lead my steps aright."

Wish I could remember that, Lord. I want to *see* the
way ahead—to *know* where I am going—to be
secure.

Then shall *I* plan the way?
Shall *I* draw up the route my life shall take?

It doesn't work, Lord.
I cannot see far enough ahead to plan.
My routes don't take me where I really want to go.

But I never learn. I blunder off on *my* path, get into
troubles, think I have learned to follow thee—and
then go blundering off on *my* path again.
You choose paths for me that I would not have chosen
for myself. They are hard paths, sometimes, and
rough, and I cannot see very far ahead. But they
always come out right, because they *are* thy paths.
To trust in thy guidance gives a transcending peace,
a sense of eternal security, an awareness of "God's
perspective" that leads my steps aright.

I don't always *need* to see.
I only need to keep walking, and trust in thee.

Amen.

Thank you, God, for little things—
    for the blessed, heart-warming little things.

I was troubled this morning—burdened—then a
meadowlark split the sky with the sheer ecstasy of
his song.
It was just a little thing—but his joy was contagious,
    and my morning took on new possibilities.

Little things, Lord. You have filled the earth with
them.
Dew on a spider's web—pussy willow—a solemn
child bearing a gift of dandelions clutched in his
fist.

A day can be dull and blind, and then a letter comes,
    a letter from a friend, and the day is light.
A day can be prosaic and ordinary,
    and one of the children, by a wink or a touch, shares
    his own inner resources, and the day is good.

Thank you, God, for little things—
        daffodils on the table, that make everyday meat
            loaf a feast,
        the smell of sheets that have hung in the sun-
            shine—
        a neighbor's cheery "hello"—
        the little miracle of new leaves,
        the gracious smile of old friends.

Thank you for the blessed, unexpected bonuses of
little things.

                        Amen.

Lord, I am afraid of the dark.

It's like when I was little, in my room at night all by
   myself—a room strange and unfamiliar because of
   the blackness—because of the frightful unknowns
   hiding in the shadows.

The "darks" are different now, Lord.
But the feeling is the same.
I am afraid of the unknowns,
and I am afraid of the fear.

The "darks" are different, now.
Sometimes I find myself afraid of tomorrow—afraid
   it will bring problems I can't cope with, or troubles
   I haven't the strength to bear. Afraid tomorrow
   will ask too much of me.
I am afraid of today's unknowns, too.
Of new people, and what they are going to think of
   me; of new paths, and where they are going to lead.
   Sometimes my fears are nameless, Lord—
   vague, unsettling, nameless fears.

When I was little and alone, the dark was to fear.
But when someone held my hand—someone tall, and
   loving, and unafraid—then the night held no terror.

Ah, Lord. So simple. I *still* need someone tall and
   loving and unafraid to hold my hand.
I still need thee.

> Thou art with me, Lord.
> And I am not afraid.

Amen.

"He leadeth me."

That hymn keeps running through my mind.
I like what it says.

It just isn't so, Lord.
You would lead me, if I let you.
And we could go farther that way.

But I keep tugging loose, like an impatient child,
and running ahead—
sure that *I* know the way I want to go.
(Perhaps half afraid you might not let me go this way,
if I waited for you.)
      Running ahead—
      into a brick wall.

That hymn ought to have another stanza, Lord.
"He followeth me."
When I go tearing off on my own, like a child, you
follow—patiently, lovingly, like a parent.
Shaking your head, Lord?
Wondering if I'll ever learn how *not* to run into brick
    walls?

You lead, when I am willing, Lord,
but the wondrous part is that you follow, when I am
not.
You follow, you find me—
      dust me off, comfort me,
      lift me up, challenge me,
      and take my hand.

               Amen.

Lord, it would be simpler if you would just let me
    be Christian on my own terms.
I prefer a *respectable* Christianity, a clean-hands Chris-
tianity that doesn't step too far out of line.
It is nice to be noble, Lord, but I surely don't want
to be conspicuous.
If I am to help with the redemption of souls, let me
    redeem those with lesser sins—and leave the dregs
    to someone else.
Lord, I *like* being respectable.
I *like* living in a clean house, in a *good* neighborhood,
calling on nice people, and having nice people call
    on me.
It would be nice if all thy children could be re-
    spectable.

Father, forgive.
My soul is full of weeds.
Jesus ate with publicans,
        visited with sinners,
        ministered to the needs of Samaritans.
Respectable folks stood aghast at the things he said
and did,
At the inappropriate, splendid things he said and did.

Father, what I *really* want is to be splendid, to do the
hard, against-the-grain and splendid thing, for thee.
Even if it makes me a misfit.

Blessed are thy nonconformists,
        for theirs is the blueprint of the kingdom.

Amen.

Thank you, God, for God.

You could have made a world like a well-run clock—
   where all you had to do was wind it now and then,
   give it a little oil, and leave it alone.
Where every gear, every cog had its job, knew its
   place, and functioned smoothly.
You could have made a world like that.

I am humbly glad you didn't.
Glad you gave us freedom to choose—to *be*.
For how could a cog feel the radiant joy that some-
   times happens to this living soul?
A cog could be created by a clocksmith.
But I was created by the living Lord, with whom I
   have fellowship.
A wheel goes neatly round and round,
but I can go off on wild flights of my own.
Or I can rise to heights beyond my ability to compre-
   hend—to thee.

You are at work in the world. Now.
You are the loving purpose that maintains order in
   the universe.
You are the irresistible force that calls this free but
   restless, yearning soul to thee.
Thank you, God, for God.

                    Amen.

I'm burdened down, Lord.

Housewifing is a long and lonely task.
When I think about all the dishes I have yet to wash,
and the meals I have yet to cook,
and the beds to make, and the floors to mop,
the day-after-day, year-after-year jobs—
it's enough to make a body weep!
It is not just "oppressed by things undone,"
but oppressed by things yet to do!

Silly, isn't it! As though I really *had* to wash all the
future's dishes today.
You send us our days one at a time, Lord.
That is all we have to cope with.
Just *this* day. And really, it isn't half bad.
A normal number of normal chores—
and in between the chores, surprises!
Some I sandwich in myself, like a minute at the piano,
or a story with the kids.
Others just happen, but they brighten the day.

Housewifing is a challenge, Lord,
    and it *can* be a pursuit.

Forgive me my tedium.
Help me take charge of my days—
    and give them all I've got.
I shall make the tools of my trade implements of
    worship, and even as I stand at the stove,
        praise thee.

Amen.

Radiance, Lord!
That is what I see sometimes.
An ordinary soul,
shining with an inner glow,
   as though a star burned somewhere in her eyes.

What gives that shine?
Part of it is joy—
      not a pollyanna optimism,
      more than a cheery grin.
Joy. *Radiant* joy.

Part of it is love, for a *self-conscious* joy lacks the
   luster. It is a shared, love-overflowing joy that shines.
Part of it is tears, or an overcoming of tears, for a real
   scaling of the heights is only accomplished by those
   who have walked their lonesome valleys.
Part of it is a nothing-held-backness.

Radiance is all-the-way involvement in something—
      no, Lord—in Someone
      who is unbounded joy
      and unlimited love.
All-the-way involvement in thee.

Radiance *is* thee, shining through.
Sometimes I see it, Lord.
Someday, perhaps, if I walk closely enough to thee,
I may even *feel* some of thy loving, radiant joy
shine through me.
For this I pray.

                    Amen.

Love is a vague, ambiguous, meaningless, worn-out
word!
There, I've said it.
It's too bad, really—
that soap operas and advertising gimmicks have "be-
littled" the word love.
It's too bad, Lord, that I can use it in such vague and
meaningless ways.

"Greater love hath no man than this, that a man lay
down his life for his friends."

A homemaker too, Lord, could have that greater love.
What more appropriate place for "agape"—for selfless,
Godlike, *greater* love—than home?

Bogged down in a word, Lord. What does it mean?

Love is action. Busywork, Lord? Or is it, when the
neighbor's kids are giving me fits, going out and
teaching them how to play marbles? Stooping to
help. Reaching to help. Running to help.
Love is waiting too. It is letting her do it herself, when
it would be easier to take over. It is sensing another's need soon enough to *not* rush in.
Love is a *hard* word, Lord. It is firmness and decision,
discipline, and maybe even harsh justice.
Love is a *soft* word, to. It is comfort and approval—a
look, a smile, the touch of a hand.
And love is knowing when to be hard and when to
be soft, when to step in and when to wait.

Ah, Lord, *love* is a vital, purposeful, splendid, brand-
new word!

Amen.

Dear Lord,

I come to thee to pray.
And don't know how—
And don't know what to say.

I am not even sure just what prayer *is*,
I only know I have this *need* to pray.
And so I kneel. And wonder what to say.

Is prayer a speech? A set of words to say?
No, Lord. To memorize a speech
And say it then, as prayer, would not mean much
To thee—or even me.

If not a speech, is prayer a time of day?
A special time I set aside to pray?
No, Lord. This time for prayer each day
Has come to mean a lot to me
Because it is a time to stop and think—
And often, when I think with thee, I pray.
Not always. For sometimes I don't get through.
Just coming, at a special time of day
Doesn't *always* mean that I can pray.

And prayer is not a debt I ought to pay.
I owe you much. I owe you all—and yet
I know that prayer is not some sort of debt.

What is prayer? Dear Lord, I think I see.
It is an answer to thy calling love.
It is communing, God within and God above.
For what is prayer but fellowship with thee.

Amen.

Who's going to come first, Lord,
Me? or thee?

Thee sounds better.
But you know how it really works out.

Pray, as long as the time, and the topic, are of my own
 choosing. As long as I do all the talking, and you
 don't say anything that disturbs me.
Serve, as long as the project is one that appeals to *me,*
 and not the sort that might soil my hands or tarnish
 my respectability.
Give, as long as it's surface giving, and as long as it's
 something I don't really need.
Love, as long as I get to choose the ones on whom I
 shall bestow my charitable love.
That's the way it goes, Lord.

Without thee, it can never be otherwise.
Without thee, *I* can never be otherwise.
Without thee, I have a small and squeezed-up heart.

I have tried to be otherwise, Lord—in bits and snatches.
But I keep drifting back to "me first."
If I could really put thee first.
Ah, Lord, if I could *really* put thee first!

Perhaps I cannot long sustain this moment of dedication.
But for an hour, Lord, for the next hour, I shall put
 thee—thee, first.

Amen.

Thee—and me—and mine.
Seems like that is mostly what I pray about, Lord.
My relationship to thee. *My* relationship to mine.
Me and *mine*. But what about *thine?*

My world gets small, and bound.
The rest of mankind seems so depersonalized
that I hug my family all the closer,
clutching at this intimacy, ignoring the rest.
Part of it is not wanting to be hurt.
To love is to become vulnerable.
Part of it is not wanting to get involved.
Not wanting to feel any responsibility for other people,
for their problems—for the cause of them, or the cure
    for them.
Part of it—you know, Lord—part of it is selfishness.

Thee—and me—and thine.
The relationship is inescapable. The involvement is
    already there.
Because all people are thy children—
    the ones I know and like,
    the ones I don't know,
    the ones I don't like,
    the ones I don't want to like,
    they are all my brothers.
This is not something I can take or leave; this is just
    something that is.
Brothers. One has a loyalty to brothers. A love. A
for-real concern.
And a just as real need for *their* love and concern.
    My heart is small, Lord.
    But because you love us all,
    I can learn to love.

        Amen.

"This is the day which the Lord hath made!"

I could tell it was going to be, Lord.
I woke up, anticipating!
And you know that is not my usual early-morning
    attitude.
And the day has *flown* by.
Good ones do.
It's the out-of-sorts days that drag.

This is the day that you have made.
        I have rejoiced in it.
        I have been glad in it.
I have even done a few things that I think you have
    approved of.
Nothing great, Lord, just a few little loving things.

This is the way you make *each* new day!
Same dazzling sun, same smell of morning.
Same space of time, filled with the promise of all the
    endless possibilities that a new day *can* hold.

This day, I could tell, was of thee.
I could tell because of the attitude of anticipation.
Let me face all my days like that, Lord—on tiptoe.
        Let me rejoice in them.
        Let me be glad in them.
For all the days of our lives are of thee.

                                        Amen.

I'm miffed, Lord.
I have been unkindly treated.
You know that.
My feelings have been trod upon,
    and they still hurt.
I'm mad.
And I have a right to be!
She shouldn't have said the things she did.
She really shouldn't.

It's kind of hard to pray, Lord,
    when I am all tied up in knots of resentment.
It is hard to think on eternals
    when my mind is all wrapped up in—in what, Lord?
In the trivial? In little peeves, and unholy resentments?
How small can I get?
Shall I let thoughtless words rob me of my self-
    possession?
Shall I allow an unkindness to spoil my day?
Such a little thing, to tear me up so.

Here. I'll spread it out and look at it.
And look at me.

Father, forgive.
And let me forgive. She did not intend to tread upon
    my sensitivity.
The sin was mine.
Father, forgive my unforgiveness.
Forgive my resenting.
The sin was mine.

Amen.

Not enough, Lord.

It's just not enough.

I visited my sick neighbor, and I took her a good pot of soup.

But what she really needed was someone to stay and talk as well.

I visited another, and talked awhile, when what she really needed was someone to bring her a good pot of soup.

Never enough, it seems like.

I do a little dab of good,
  and quit, just before I have really *contributed*.

Like when I made my child a new dress, Lord, and what she really needed was my help on a new philosophy.

I guess it is the second mile.

The first one is required—
  a feeling of "Well, I really *ought* to do that much."

But to go further—
  I don't think of it.

To do more—
  I don't bother.

Lord, you didn't ask me to do "little dabs" of kindness.

You didn't promise me a nice, pleasant, easy go of it.

You said, "Be perfect." And were.

            "Go further." And went.

            "Do more." And did.

Little dabs aren't enough.

Half-hearted won't get the job done.

Lord, let every tick of the kitchen clock remind me of the *challenge*,

the hard, demanding *challenge*
  of your way of life.

Amen.

Lord, Lord,

Listen, I pray,
And give me right words
to use today.
>Let the chastening I must do
>be gently done.
>Let the instructing I must say
>be gently said.
Let me remember to be kind.

So easily I use a barbed and thoughtless word.
So readily I tread with heavy foot and sightless eyes
into a moment of awe and wonder.

Sightless eyes.
Kindness is *seeing*, Lord—
>commending the worthy,
>ignoring the thoughtless,
>uplifting the feeble attempts at greatness.
Kindness is seeing,
>and not seeing.

Let me, this day, have *kind* eyes,
>and gentle hands,
that I may not squelch a child experimenting with
thought,
nor startle one confronted with beauty.
Let me walk cautiously, gently,
>and be kind.

Amen.

What am I, Lord?
Lowborn worm, groveling in the dust? (I don't care
  for that a bit.)
Or partaker of the divine nature? (I don't measure
  up to *that*.)
Who am I, Lord?
     You know,
     but I don't.
You see through the masks I wear,
  but I hide me, even from myself.
Masks of respectability.
  Their mother. *His* wife. Roles. And masks.

I'm Everyman, Lord—
  product of all that has gone before,
  sum of all that I have known.
But I'm different, too.
A combination of genes that never happened before,
  and will not happen again. An individual, the
  likes of which there is none other.
Give me the courage to strip off the masks, Lord,
  and be *me*.
Wait—not a lawless, selfish me.
Give me the courage to strip off the masks and be
  thine.
Only once, only this once, did you create a me.
Now let me *use* this unique life, for thee.

Just words? I hide behind words like I hide behind
  masks.
     Who am I, Lord?
     Who am I?

               Amen.

What is it, Lord—
    this disquiet within—
for life is good,
    and of thee.
My days follow each other in only mild disorder.
Seasons come, and go,
and I know they will continue to do so.
I have work to do,
work that I feel is significant—

Why, then?
Why this discontent?
This restlessness?

This, too, is of thee.

Because you have shown me how life can be lived by
a Son of God—
because you have offered me, too, sonship—
I cannot be content with this present me.
You offer me high adventure,
    here, where I am,
    within the dailiness of my own living.
That's what I want, Lord—
    high adventure,
    high surrender—
    the nothing-held-backness of walking with thee.

For this—for thee,
    I am restless.
My reach exceeds my grasp,
but Lord, I reach for thee.

                    Amen.

Father, forgive my withholdings.

I don't mind offering to thee
  a portion of myself,
for I like to think of myself as belonging to thee.
I don't mind offering to thee
  a measure of my service,
for I like to think of myself as compassionate.

But Lord, forgive my withholdings.
Forgive, that I have kept back.
My generosity has been apportioned.
My dedication has been a halfway thing.
Then I begrudge the little I have given,
and complain of the cost of following thee.

Forgive my withholding, Lord.
Whether I hold back out of shyness—
  ("Shyness" has a respectable ring;
  the *right* word is "selfishness," isn't it, Lord?)
or out of fear, that the cost might deprive me of
  something,
or out of the denseness of a mind that does not really
  want to understand.

Forgive my withholdings.
Forgive my begrudgings.
Let there be no piecemeal dedication,
but take me as I am, Lord, and make of me something
  useful.
Use *all* of me; and in the *glory* of following thee,
  who shall count the cost?

                        Amen.

Lord, send me a sense of urgency.

Time is running out on me.
Not tomorrow, or next month—
   but the time that I have with these my children
   is running out on me.
They will soon be too big for fairy tales and sunset
   walks—
too big to squat down beside me by the flower bed,
   to admire the progress of an inchworm.
Too big, and too occupied with their peers.

Time is running out, and there are so many things I
   have yet to teach them.
Lord, they must come to know thee.
And to love thee.
And to feel a belongingness to thee.
This is not something I can *give* them.
But Lord, help me show them how it is with thee and
   me.

They have such big choices to make, these next years.
Help me guide them toward the spiritual maturity
   from which such choices can be wisely made.
Let me not be afraid to say to them,
        "God made this—
         God did this—
         It is God who makes us feel this way."
Time is running out, Lord.
And there are so many things I need to tell them.
How shall I say them, Lord?
What shall I say?

                    Amen.

Oh, me of little faith!
I make long lists of things I must get done—
    little, piddling *self* things.
Was it for *this* that I was born into the world?

Lord, let me get hold of something *big,*
and steadfastly see it through.

Father who made me,
    who sustains me,
        who will, if I permit it, lead me to things beyond
        myself,
let me believe bigger—
step off on newer, harder paths,
knowing that if I stumble, *thou dost not fall!*
Let me believe bigger.

The size of the universe is beyond all telling of it,
    and you are Lord of all that.
The possibilities of a single soul—even one like me—
    staggers the imagining,
because you are Lord of us, too.

Why should I fret and stew over *little* things?
I am apprenticed to the living Lord!
Failures behind me,
inadequacies confronted,
I am apprenticed to the living Lord.

                    Amen.

Lord, I sometimes get the feeling that when I come
    to this place of quiet to pray—
well, I ought to somber-up a little!
What a curious misconception—that Christianity
    should be a sober-sided affair.

It is *laughter* you love, Lord!
It is overflowing, uncontainable joy.

Where does it come from, this holy joy?
It comes from thee.
From a faith in the ultimate rightness of life.
From a surrender of worries and anxieties over the
    joy-robbing *little* things.
Sometimes it comes from a fragment of beauty, too
    lovely to overlook.
Mostly it comes from an awareness of being part of
    something
        bigger than I am—
        something tremendous,
        and jubilant.

Somber? Not so, Lord.
Drab? Not thee, Lord.
Dull? Not me, Lord,
        not if I let myself be caught up in thy holy joy!

Amen.

I was looking for a scapegoat, Lord.
And I took it out on her.

My feelings were hurt.
Did I really think it would help matters to hurt hers,
    too?

Why *do* I hurt the ones I love?
So deliberately, sometimes, Lord.
Gouging into the tenderness of their feelings,
    because I am too preoccupied to care.

I hurt them because I am impatient—
        impatient with their imperfections,
        impatient with their immaturities,
        impatient with their necessity to be themselves.
I hurt them because I misunderstand.
I misunderstand their purposes.
And it is not a casual failure to fathom—
but an *unwillingness* to admit they might *have* a point.

I lash out at those I would protect.
I lambast those whom I would love.
I hurt—and see them cringe—and hurt again.
Lord, when I see what I am doing,
why can't I stop?

Lord, I pray for these whom I love.
For these whom I hurt *because* I love them.
Let my love be great enough to overcome myself.
Let me love them unselfishly, and for their own sakes.
        And Lord, let me not hurt them so.

Amen.

Lord, bless my tedium.

A certain amount of it has just got to be.
Same old beds—thank you, Lord, for a place to lay
our heads.
Same old dishes—thank you, Lord, for food to eat.
Same old dailiness. And thank you, Lord, for the
security of daily jobs to do!

Thou, Lord, creator of all the mighty universe, art
also God of the common things,
the homely, homey common things.
Let me delight in them.
Let me find little pleasures in them—
in the sparkle of glass,
and the smoothness of wood,
and the smell of sunshine in the house.

And if I tie a shoe a thousand times,
let me remember to show him I enjoy tying his
shoes—
let me enjoy also teaching him to do it for himself.
Tedium? Not really, Lord.
For thou art God of the common things of the common day.

And if thou art with me,
here in the routine of my common day,
how shall any task seem trivial?

Lord, bless with thy presence my tedium.

Amen.

Lord, deliver me from triteness.

From small talk—at a time when significant things
    need to be said.
From trivialities—at a time when significant things
    need to be done.

Deliver me from the pettiness that blinds me to
    desperate need in another,
who also covers up with small talk.

Why am I afraid to speak of eternals—
    even to a friend, or to my child,
    who yearns *to be able* to speak of such things?
Is it because I am not enough at home with thee
    myself,
and am afraid someone else might see the smallness
    of my own faith?
So I let the tender moment pass—with a remark about
    the weather.

Lord, deliver me from triteness.
Give me the wisdom—
    yes, and the *courage*—
    to be significant when it matters.
Give me the intuitive awareness of another's
    reaching out to communicate.

And deliver me from triteness.

                                        Amen.

What is it, Lord, to be "called"?

For Paul, it was voices, and a great light from heaven.

But I don't hear any voices. I don't see any visions.
This is what I *wish* would happen—
    a direct communication.
It would be so much easier if I knew, for *sure,* what
    you want me to do.
Beyond any shadow of a doubt.
Like voices I can hear, Lord.
Like a vision.

And yet, I know.
I get my call—and it is just as surely from thee
    as though it were an engraved invitation.
I just don't want to recognize it.
My call is a feeling of "oughtness."
A recognition of a need—
    an awareness that I could do something about it.
This is my kind of call.

And it is from thee—just as surely as the visions and
    voices.

To cultivate an ear that hears,
and an eye that sees,
and a heart atune to "oughtness,"
is to grow closer to thee.
This, in itself, becomes direct communication.
        Thank you, God.

                Amen.

109

Father, it is for the youth I pray.
For those on the road to becoming,
here in this household,
and here in this community.

You understand their growing pains, Lord.
Help *me* understand.
I nag and criticize—
    which doesn't uplift them.
I am guilty of musty moralizing,
    which doesn't undergird them.

They need undergirding, Lord.
They feel the pressures of maturity,
    with which they are not yet able to cope.
They feel half-child, half-grown, half-nothing.
They need thy undergirding.
        Give them patience, Lord.
        Give them obedience and humility.
        Give them energy and joy.
    Give them a heart full of gladness.

Lord, I pray for the youth.
But I pray for me, too.
These are exactly the things *I* need—
        Undergirding.
        Patience.
        Obedience, and humility.
        Energy, and joy.
Give us understanding, Lord, and a heart full of
    gladness.

                        Amen.

110

Lord, deliver me from my little gods.

You know the things I worship.
The things I give my thoughts to,
      my time to,
      my heart to.
You know them, Lord.
Give me the gumption to know them myself,
to face them for what they are—
      little gods,
      impotent, unworthy, and *little*.

But I make *gods* of them by putting them first.
I let *things* become too important, too dominating.
I become so wrapped up in even *good* things
that I forget from whence cometh my very life!
I put my trust in little gods,
and little gods will let me down.
There is no peace, no strength, no redemption in little
      gods.

Deliver me, Lord.
No. That is too painless.
Tear me away from my little gods!
It has to be a searing, hurting severance.
Tear me away.

                    Amen.

My Father,
>in whose presence is heaven,
>holy is thy name.

May thy kingdom come now—
>>thy kingdom of heaven around me,
>>wherein I may prepare myself for heaven beyond me.

Lord, thy will be done.
>>I subject myself to thee—
>>for thou art God.

Give me this day my daily bread,
>and let me not worry about tomorrow's flour.

Give me also a compassionate awareness of those who
have no bread.

Forgive me my sins,
>against others, Lord,
>and against thee.

Forgive, and require of me a forgiveness of those who
sin against me.

Let me not court temptation, Lord,
>nor dabble in unworthy pursuits,
but deliver me from evil.

For thine is the kingdom—
>no paltry time-spanned kingdom of earth,
>but the realm eternal.

And thine is the power—*Lord, God, creator of the
ends of the earth.*

And thine is the glory,
>the radiant, exultant glory of the living Lord
>forever,
>forever.

>>>>Amen.